A Purim Story

Rachel Mintz

Once upon a time, in a small town, there was a small bakery which was known for its delicious cakes.

The baker was busy all day making cookies and ball shaped buns, feeding the ovens with sweet dough from dawn to dusk.

One morning when the baker came to the bakery he saw something strange laying on the cookies stand, a **triangle** cookie!?

He rubbed his eyes, he never saw anything like it ever before.

A Triangle cookie?

He picked it up, checked it from all sides and sniffed it. It was crumbling, with dark filling and a sweet buttery smell. The shape was not like anything he had ever seen before. "What kind of cookie is it? I have to find out!" he thought and placed the cookie on the shelf.

At noon he closed the bakery and set off to find out more about the little triangle cookie. He walked down the street asking people, showing them the small unique pastry, "have you ever seen a cookie like this? Do you know what it is?"

But no one recognized it.

"What a unique cookie" he thought.

At evening the baker decided to ask one last person, and saw an old man walking slowly toward him. He stopped him and asked, "excuse me dear sir" he raised the cookie, "do you know what is this cookie?" The man came closer.. He said, "I think I saw it once.. I am not sure.. it is some kind of Jewish cookie. I think they call it a **Matzah.**"

The baker was happy, he found out what kind of cookie it is. So you are a "**Matzah**" he thought, how nice. The baker wanted to learn more about the Matzah, so the next day he woke up early and went to the town's synagogue to ask the people there about the Matzah.

He met outside the synagogue a small kid and asked him, "can you tell me the story of the **Matzah**, why do Jews prepare it and eat it?"

The kid replied, "The Matzah is the food our people prepared when they fled from Egypt. God told them to pack and leave in such a haste they did not wait for their bread dough to rise. So since then we eat at Passover the flat, stiff Matzah."

"Flat and stiff?" the baker was puzzled, "the cookie I found had a sweet smell and had sugar powder on top." "Oh, then it must be a SufGaNiya!" the kid said, "these are made from dough and they are sweet with sugar powder on top!" He said and run away to play with his friends.

The baker was happy, he finally found out what was the name of the triangle cookie. It is a **Sufganiya**!

He went to his bakery with a wonderful idea in his head. He will examine this Jewish pastry and learn how to make it and add it as a new cookie to his bakery shelves.

When he arrived at his bakery, he too a close look at the triangle cookie, he tasted the buttery crumbling texture, licked the sweet date filling and the sugar powder above it.

He began to make his own triangle cookies!

The baker worked and worked until by noon, he had a large pile of triangle cookies. He was really proud of himself.

He updated the big sign outside the bakery with the news, he is now serving -
NEW FRESH SUFGANIYA.

People who passed by, walked in to buy and taste, they all praised the baker
for the delicate crumbling dough and sweet taste. They loved it!

The baker was standing proud at the doorstep of his bakery. When one of the kids saw the sign and burst in a roaring laughter...

"This is not a Sufganiya!!" the boy said, "the Sufgania is a doughnut, fried in deep oil, and eaten at Hanukkah... this is a *Hamantash!*"

"Haman... What??"

"Hamantash*! We eat hamantaschen at* **Purim***! They are also called Haman Ears!"*

The baker smiled when he understood what happened, the triangle cookie tricked him once again.

"Then I will have to change the sign to NEW FRESH HAMANTASCHEN," he said.

He invited the kids into his bakery "while you eat few Hamantaschen tell me all about the strange name and shape."

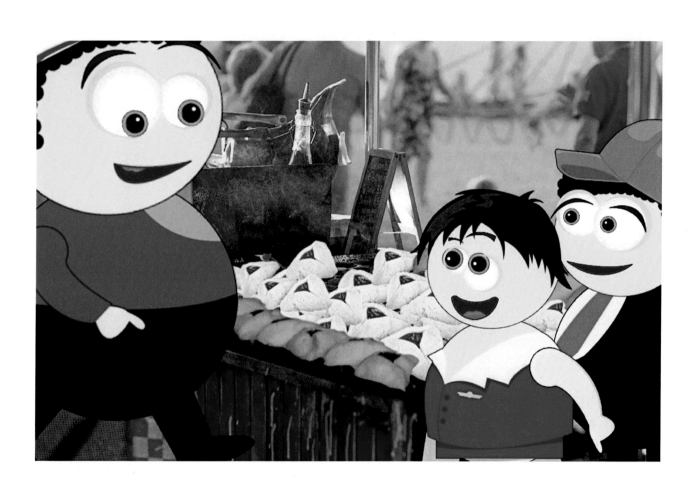

The kids told the good baker about a wicked evil man called **Haman**, who lived long ago in Persia. Haman had a plan to kill all the Jews in the kingdom at one specific day. He rolled the dice and decided his plan would take place at the 13th of the Hebrew month of Adar.

At the same time the King of Persia married a beautiful Jewish woman called **Esther.** Her uncle **Mordechai** discovered Haman's plot. With the help of Queen Esther he brought the bad news to the King, that Haman ordered to kill all the Jews of the country in one single day. When the king hears about this plot he immediately orders Haman to be hanged.

And Mordechai is led on the royal horse through the streets of the capital.

The Jews were saved!! There were huge celebrations when the plot was revealed and the threat removed. Until this day, **Purim** is celebrated with costumes, music, lots of wine and sweet triangle cookies called Hamantaschen! Haman's Ears! So we never forget Haman's plot and God's miracle to defeat it.

"That's a great story to remember!" The baker said.

He lifted a cookie, took a bite at one of the corners and said "Now thanks to you, I will not forget evil Haman either, you little sneaky tricky Hamantash."

The End

More Children Books For Purim:

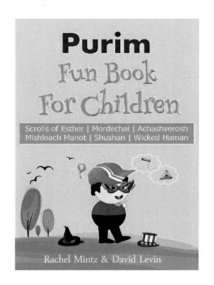

Book for kids with lots of fun activities, puzzles, mazes, and challenges about Purim. Great way to learn and remember the Purim story.

There is a Purim Party at the forest and all the animals come dressed up. A **rhyme** book for the young ones.

Order Jewish Festivals Fun Books

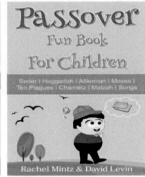

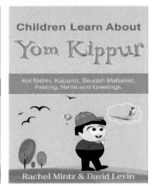

Fun way to enrich your kids about more Jewish festivals.

Learning the main themes and traditions for each festival with colorful puzzles and creative activities

Hebrew Counting Books

Learning Hebrew Alphabet & Vowels

Learn how to read Hebrew Vowels. The best book to learn Niqqud. For those who know the Hebrew Aleph-Bet.

Improve the kids Hebrew by learning with a coloring book and practice pages.

Short Story Books For Kids

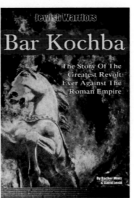

A boy deals with bullies at school like Judah Maccabee.

Passover exodus story with Zombies

The story of the legendary Bar Kochba.

Quick Decoration Kit Books

Sukkot & Hanukkah
Home, Sukkah, Classroom

A fun Jewish Tale for Rosh Hashanah

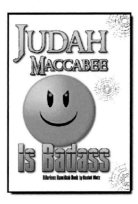

Please take a moment to leave me a review – Thanks.

Chag Purim Sameach

Rachel Mintz

Made in the USA
Middletown, DE
28 February 2018